About the Author

After my daughter was born, I began to see the world around me with a fresh pair of eyes. Her overwhelming expressions to wind, rain and even mashed sprouts reignited within me a spark to write again. I'm a dentist by trade but my passions are not contained only to my profession. Poetry became my imaginative outlet to express my musings and if it departs some wisdom to a fellow reader along the way then I count that as a personal victory!

Life's Pruning

Kuljit Kaur Grewal

Life's Pruning

Olympia Publishers
London

www.olympiapublishers.com
OLYMPIA PAPERBACK EDITION

Copyright © Kuljit Kaur Grewal 2025

The right of Kuljit Kaur Grewal to be identified as author of
this work has been asserted in accordance with sections 77 and 78 of
the Copyright, Designs and Patents Act 1988.

All Rights Reserved

No reproduction, copy or transmission of this publication
may be made without written permission.
No paragraph of this publication may be reproduced,
copied or transmitted save with the written permission of the publisher,
or in accordance with the provisions
of the Copyright Act 1956 (as amended).

Any person who commits any unauthorised act in relation to
this publication may be liable to criminal
prosecution and civil claims for damage.

A CIP catalogue record for this title is
available from the British Library.

ISBN: 978-1-83543-238-9

This is a work of fiction.
Names, characters, places and incidents originate from the writer's
imagination. Any resemblance to actual persons, living or dead, is
purely coincidental.

First Published in 2025

Olympia Publishers
Tallis House
2 Tallis Street
London
EC4Y 0AB

Printed in Great Britain

Dedication

I dedicate this book to my daughter Navneet and husband Sukhraj, who have had to endure my rhyming mutterings in the early hours of the morning!

Acknowledgements

I extend my gratitude to my parents and siblings that have shaped and encouraged me to fulfil my aspirations. Until you become a parent yourself you don't realise the countless sacrifices the previous generations have made.

Contents

Author's foreword 13
Life's Pruning 15
My voyage to immortality 17
Ageing wisdom 20
The vacant house 23
The circle of life 26
A labyrinth of infinite wisdom 28
'Love to bake' or 'bake for love' 30
At the mercy of the dating world 32
The ruthless claws of covid 36
The gilded cage of a doctor 38
The celebrity imposter 40
Autumn 42
The skeletons of Halloween 44
The old sparks of Bonfire Night 46
Winter 48
Christmas Eve in the North Pole 50
The uninvited Icy guest 54
Postpartum mum 57
First day back 59
The birth of a little boss 61
The musings of a dad 63
The loss of a little friend 64
Rules 67
The fable of inferno 71
My clever brother Tom 75

Author's foreword

The art of pruning can be easily applied to plants as put simply 'by cutting away dead or overgrown branches or stems' with the hope that the new year will bring about a new blossom. However, are we not all a product of pruning by life? Once careers are determined, the journey strips away superfluous or unwanted traits to reveal a skeleton that becomes today's unanimous workforce.

From a young age we are encouraged to explore the unknowns to expand our skills sets in the comforts of our parents or teachers' watchful supervision. However, what was once significant facts dwindles away to the abyss once a career path is embarked.

We all remember regurgitation of timetables, rote learning of mathematical formulae and paraphrasing of Shakespeare works, however how much of that is applicable to today's world. Do we as adults selectively prune away the knowledge that once shaped our childhood?

The recent birth of my daughter has taught me the meaning of unconditional love but also to see the world with a fresh pair of eyes. As a parent you succumb to their demands as let's face it, they do have the upper hand!

This anthology is testament that never feels your previous knowledge has been lost, for it only takes a moment to walk down memory lane and cherish that time of innocence that was once in your grasp. For even if for a second if the assistance of this mere book allows you to loiter back into your childhood bliss than that in itself is priceless!

Life's Pruning

Standard deviation, Pythagoras theory and Algebra all fundamental branches of mathematics,
the teenager in me scribbles down frantically calculating the value of x in a class full of fanatics.
Now I struggle to do basic arithmetic at the supermarket checkout,
thinking will I have enough for that Snickers bar that I cannot do without.

Onomatopoeia, pathetic fallacy and Iambic pentameter the English teacher preaches,
as the child in me fingers the pages of Macbeth hoping to remember the lengthy speeches.
Now as I skim through the daily Metro newspaper on my tiring work commute,
my mind wonders whether Shakespeare himself knew the amount of readers he would one day recruit.

Photosynthesis, homeostasis and respiration all essential to biological existence,
as the child in me waters my sunflower seeds diligently hoping it provides substance.
Now as I idly loiter through the garden centre screening for perennial flowers,
my mind wonders if they will survive in the upcoming rainy

showers.

Gravity, momentum and Newton's Laws I recite off the top of my head,
whereas once as a child the mere thought of physics was one to dread.
Now as a mother I watch my child throw water balloons carefree,
all the while thinking the apple doesn't fall far from the tree.

Isotopes, Nomenclature and periodic tables resonates the elements in life,
each with its unique bonding and behavioural rife.
Now as I await for the pharmacist to hand over my regular medicines,
I struggle to write their lengthy names, thinking thank God for the development of colchicine!

For in each stage of life we usurp the knowledge flowing,
all the while forgetting that some is transiently foregoing.
As we mature, our choices prune away mastered skills,
becoming a unanimous workforce that obediently follows the drills.

But where once we chased optimistic grades,
we now become our own specialised trades.
Each decision carving our own individual trajectory,
so that one day we succeed to be found in the phonebook directory!

My voyage to immortality

So how does one defeat death and achieve infinite immortality,
Don't get me wrong I have planted my seed all thanks to my quirky personality!
But what's to say the procreation cycle will transcend through the ages,
as finding a mating partner is down to chance, biology and likely financial wages!
And with that what's to say the next generation will produce the finest biological specimens,
That will overcome hardships and resist environmental struggles and evade diseases by dosing up on lecithin!

So it got me researching as we all know the Philosopher Stone has been destroyed,
And recreating magical stones is beyond my remit even if I consult my good friend Freud.
So I decide to pester my GP who raised her eyebrows in surprise,
For surely anything short than a psychiatric referral would be advised.
In summary she concluded a good diet, regular exercise and medication would be wise.
So this got me thinking to consult the gods above as surely religion holds some insightful surmise.

Finally my eye came upon Buddhism and reincarnation of the spirit in a cyclic manner,
But the thought of coming back as an ant would be a bummer in my life planner.
So I went back to the drawing board, how to preserve oneself that is immune to time,
Surely cryogenic freezing would preserve me in my prime?
If one was to freeze their body to halt the biological process,
Then future medical technology could restore health presumably, warranting it to be a success!
But if Darwin's theory is correct 'survival of the fittest' then would my outdated body suffice,
Would I be at a disadvantage compared to my successors that have not been trapped in ice?

Exasperated I decided to watch some football to take my mind off things,
These talented chaps kicking a ball around will have no shortage of flings.
That's it! If I create a name for myself by showcasing an extraordinary talent then I could become the incredible Frank!
But I'm not a good runner, neither a computer geek and dancing well that depends on the number of pints drank!

So I sit in the library idly wondering if life is in fact a short-lived bliss with finite days,
For death is an untimely guest that greets everyone when it's time to exit life's maze.
I meander through the aisles, the diary of Anne Frank is

evidence that death has a cruel unpredictable course,
Sitting opposite is Gandhi teachings that have permeated through the years with inaudible force.
'For an eye for an eye leaves the whole world blind', is how I break up pubs brawls.
Then it hits me the 'pen is mightier than the sword' for I write animatedly in my scrawl,
'My voyage on how to obtain immortality' so that future generations may benefit from my musings,
I have created this work for your perusing so that someone one day may find me amusing!

Ageing wisdom

Staring at the ceiling, I recall these same eyes once scrutinised the works of Gaudi,
Whereas these fingers once caressed the slick steering wheel of an Audi.
Now neither function at their best as reading glasses perch on the bridge of my nose,
And my swollen joints ache as Gout has taken hold of my toes.

A chill in the air makes me button up my frilly nightgown.
These bosoms now retired from their nursing days as breastmilk was once letdown,
Now they stand testament to gravity as the reality of menopause reared its ugly head,
With the hot flushes and sleep disturbances cursing one to a restless bed.

My wedding ring flashes in the sunlight, witness to the vows recited in our prime,
Till death do us part was but a distant memory for exchange of this dime.
For cancer was the culprit that separated two connected souls,
Allowing one to depart contently whilst the other made peace with these four walls.

For on that day, desolation was my only companion as he uttered his last breath,
The morning newspaper and a cup of tea was his morning routine until his untimely death.
Now the newspapers pile up in an unceremonious clutter,
As I refuse to allow them to be disposed of until I hear his angelic mutter.

Now as the days merge into one another I pass time submerged in my memories,
Tracing the outlines of my glass menagerie set and ornamental accessories.
For each figurine has sentimental value and an associated sacred story,
Take for example the horseshoe trinket gifted on my wedding day reminds me of the day's grandeur and glory,
The glass angel figurine was always to be handled with care, a tiny delicate thing,
I bought this after my miscarriage to console my heart, if only God hadn't gifted him wings.

Now in this large house I potter along surrounded by my child's memorabilia,
each a prized relic that tell the childhood tale of my daughter Amelia.
For now she too has flown the nest and is navigating the journey of motherhood,
Teaching her offspring good discipline whilst lavishing their innocent childhood.

The doorbell rings announcing the arrival of the weekly shopping,
I open the door to welcome the delivery man who is fast in his hasty dropping.
To be able to move so agilely was a blessing in itself allowing one a prompt attendance,
as nowadays I rely on my walking stick as my friend to sustain my independence.

I fish through the shopping searching for my trusted marmalade as that spread on toast is my favourite meal,
Whereas once it was a Sunday roast, bargaining with the little one to finish her vegetables was always quite an ordeal!
Now with my sparse teeth I slobber through what I can,
For whatever quenches the hunger pangs is better than munching pecans.

I glance outside the window watching life go by, the moving vehicles and laughter of children is a merry sight,
wishing to be that nine-year-old boy that lavishes his ice cream with such delight.
Remembering that every day was a blessing of this fulfilling life,
As one is unable to be reborn and relive it twice.
So enjoy the good with the bad as every life is a glorious celebration,
For once we enter the casket we are at our final destination.

The vacant house

It all started with an ultrasound confirming the patter of feet arriving imminently soon.
Followed by the apartment overflowing with gifts on arriving back from the babymoon.
Then the panic of house searching to accommodate the paraphernalia associated with baby care,
For most of our furniture was second-hand or worn and carpets threadbare.
Finally after several house viewings we came across a house that met the specifications,
With its picket white fence, manicured lawn and open kitchen plan being the hotspot for conversations.
As the months passed my belly grew and paperwork was complete,
Progressing to moving in day when we became familiar to the new street.

Then the euphoria came of collecting keys and taking the signature photo to signpost our new buy,
For our forever home was now officially ours to populate ready for our due date in July.
Locks were changed, curtains were bought for security and privacy were our first thought,
Followed by the installation of a new fridge so consumables were not spoilt in fraught.

Then when boxes were unloaded we sat on the floorboards assessing the empty canvas of each room,
Imagining how each will manifest with our personal touch into its own homely bloom.

Settling into our new house was enthralling at first exploring its depths and intricacies,
then came the creaking of floorboards and eerie shadows hindering nighttime intimacies.
For a sparsely furnished house looks forlorn but with limited funds it would have to suffice,
With each passing month another item of furniture arrived at a fair price,
with the inflatable mattress stowed away to make room for a new family bed and cot.
Followed by kitchen utensils unboxed and sanitised ready to cook chicken hotpot!

Walls were stripped bare and painted in a warm vibrance,
As heating systems were upgraded for energy compliance.
Baby gifts were washed, dried and stashed away,
ready for the new arrival that could come any day.
Then the day materialised when a new inhabitant carved its way to dominate,
As the house became animated with life as godparents were shortlisted to nominate.

Christmas trees were adorned and fireplaces lit to bask in its comforting warmth,
For the vacant house had transformed to a welcoming sanctuary henceforth.

Finally becoming a family home that is cluttered with furnishings and possessions that is surplus to say at best. For the circle of life has us lodge several transient guests even those uninvited that become annoying household pests!

The circle of life

Muffins for gran, cinnamon swirls for Jess and a maraca for my baby niece,
For any more cooking and I would surely become obese.
My first pitstop was to drop off the swirls with my sister who recently gave birth to a baby girl,
For a little sugar and chatter will definitely uplift her spirit especially once she sinks her teeth into a sweet swirl.
My niece breaks into a smile and arches her back jumping in surprise,
For walking was a stretch for now as she was dribbling mothereses in replies.

After a while, I departed enroute to the nursing home where Gran resides,
On entering her eyes lit up as her vision recognised those she prides.
Her dementia meant that her short term memory wasn't its best,
But yet she still could regurgitate her childhood details as if it was a test.
Blueberry muffins were her favourite as she takes a bite with her dentures,
Dribbling a little as she recalls her youthful adventures.

That night I was lost in thought, as my mind processed the

day's activities,
For wasn't life ironic? A transient journey of achieving milestones and partaking in annual joyous festivities.
Only for one day those learned skills and knowledge to unravel, losing each mastered capability,
Stripping away independence, autonomy and security reducing us to a liability.

As a baby we are restricted to a liquid diet for dentition is yet to appear,
Once we lose our teeth we fall back to liquids for dentures can barely spear.
As a baby walking unaided is a challenge as we wobble with hands outstretched,
Once arthritis strikes we rely on walking sticks to precariously hobble proving to be too far stretched.
As a baby we urinate and excrete at our will without any hesitation,
Once incontinence strikes, diapers are a necessity for basic sanitation.

As a baby our vision is blurred as we rely on smells and contrast to guide us to our mother's arms,
Only for later our vision to degenerate leading us dependent on glasses to read our alarms.
For as a baby we struggle to compose sentences resorting to incomprehensible babbling,
However an untimely stroke has us verbally impaired with slurred words being our best scrambling.
As a baby we enter wrapped up in a blanket in a Moses basket,
Only to leave dressed in our finery in an elegantly adorned open casket.

A labyrinth of infinite wisdom

As a child, my favourite place has always been the library,
It was always the awaited stop in my weekly itinerary.
A plethora of great minds laid bare in the pages of every book,
Waiting to depart their wisdom selflessly for those that look.

Each sector containing a captivating genre waiting to cocoon those that believe,
From fiction to autobiographies for those searching in the past for answers to retrieve.
Each page bringing to life the characters contained within,
So one might immerse themselves in an utopia therein.

The fantasy world of fiction offers one escapism from reality,
For the authors have created a legacy that surpasses mortality.
The musings of Roald Dahl were my prized possessions,
The cracked spines of his books evidence to my childhood obsession.

As I grew older, I loitered in the old-time classics of the Bronte sisters admiring their hidden talent,
Their isolated settings and Byronic heroes were no less than gallant.

Now as time surpasses these books will be iconic for preserving the patriarchal times,
For now society has been shaped by moving culture and punishes those that commit such crimes.

The fantasy world of J.R.R Tolkien was enlightening to the youngest minds,
From its little hobbits to animated forests all intricately defined.
With each reader being a blank canvas awaiting the author to paint a masterpiece of their kind,
So that one can truly become submerged in an illusion detached from their daily grind.

The gothic horror genre is one that will have you quivering in your boots,
For Oscar Wilde's Dorian Gray shows even a portrait can deteriorate with sinful acts in cahoots.
Mary Shelley's Frankenstein wages a battle between nature and science,
For even Victor suffers the consequences of his creation's defiance.

The power of every word is not to be underestimated as each holds a significance,
For the author has injected their soul into every page with due diligence.
Therefore the next time you embark across the threshold of a library do turn back,
For there at your fingertips is the strength of infinite minds awaiting to enter your rucksack.

'Love to bake' or 'bake for love'

So my mother always said the way to a man's heart is through his belly,
So I started my cooking journey to ensure I could make more than just wobbly jelly.
So I start with the assistance of my mother to bake a Victoria sponge cake,
For her elegance and passion in baking was second to none make no mistake.
But also her anxiety in seeing me in the kitchen alone was enough for her to partake,
As I rummaged for mixing bowls and spatulas sounding no less than an earthquake.
So we cream the butter and caster sugar together until it's fluffy and light,
My mother radiates innate grace whilst I hammer at the butter defiantly with all my might.
Next she hands me the egg carton which is a precarious task as I raise my eyebrows in surprise,
as cracking eggs was not my strength unless broken shells were to be the secret ingredient in disguise.
With a little luck I blend the eggs after checking for hidden shell fragments with a whisk,
Following which she swiftly beats in the eggs incrementally producing an aerated homogenous mix.
Next she provides me with a bag of flour and sieve as I turn

to her with my sheepish grin,
She rolls her eyes demonstrating effortlessly how to fold the flour gently in.
With that it was ready to bake as I pour the contents into a cake tin.
For the end product was delicious to say the least as I celebrated my well-deserved win.
For I was filled with admiration for my mother as baking is truly a skilled art,
However I hang up my apron and resign as I work better as the food connoisseur counterpart.

Call it experience honed by years of practice or innate skill,
But there's just somethings I would rather leave to the experts and pay the bill,
As let's be honest any fruits of my labour would likely be detrimental to one's health to savour!

At the mercy of the dating world

So here I find myself swiping right or left to find a match,
Fishing through a sea of faces hoping to find a good catch!
But to reduce a person to a picture and a list of attributes is belittling,
As let's be honest it's our unique quirks that makes us all riveting.

But after several fruitless conversations nothing materialised,
So here I find myself at a speed dating event dressed to impress as advertised.
With my best foot forward I muddle through topics of discussion to prioritise,
For we all have dealbreakers and pet hates that we deeply despise.

So it begins with a chime of bell as chairs are arranged in a concentric fashion,
As rotations are explained and slips of paper are distributed with compassion.
After each chime a new suitor presents, each exchanging formalities at best,
For how much can one divulge in three minutes to create a lasting impression is the test!

After several feigned smiles the bell chimes announcing break time,
Naturally the ladies gravitate to the toilets awaiting to discuss those in their prime.
Whilst I search for my phone hoping to distract myself away from this contrived setting,
I scan around the room assessing the candidates subconsciously vetting.
Looking around the guys stand in clusters discussing other worldly affairs,
How is one supposed to make conversation when all appear deep in their amicable pairs?
I curse my mother's persuasive words "One has to kiss a few frogs before you find your prince."
Surely no knight in shining armour will loiter past this elaborate threshold I wince.

The bell chimes again, time to regroup and meet the next lot,
I scramble back placing the first round's paper in its allocated slot.
So it begins as false flatteries are exchanged and mutual ground is sought,
As those desperately seeking companionship become progressively fraught.

Finally after an exhausting three hours the event concludes, those with reciprocated love interests exchange numbers proving to be successful pursues.
I pack my belongings, thinking whilst some conversations were stimulating,
None ignited that well-spoken of 'spark' that would have

been fascinating.

So I drive home as my brain seeks refuge from today's numerous interactions,
As I clear my mind I search within myself what is it that I seek in a partner for my satisfaction.
Stability? Attraction? Excitement? Companionship? Honesty? Didn't sound much,
But with a world full of choices filtering through the masses it feels like such.

I exhale deeply ridden with sorrow as disappointment dawns,
For I question if love is an unattainable concept that makes one a vulnerable pawn.
I curse my tunnel vision during university as surely finding a like-minded partner would have been attainable,
But back then academic pursuits and careers prospects were just about obtainable.

I slam the brakes unceremoniously as the traffic lights rapidly flash red,
Before I know it a car crashes into my rear ripping the boot to shred.
The driver runs out frantically apologising profusely at his mistake,
In shock I gaze at him in amazement as in that moment I knew he was my big break.
And now after forty years of marriage we still believe it was fate,
After all not everyone can say a car crash scene became their

first date!

But truly love is just a word until someone comes along and gives it meaning,
However when you find that soulmate that deep connection is surreal like you are dreaming.
So a glimmer of hope for those bachelors and maidens that believe love is fake,
For here stands a lady that is smitten and forever will be indebted to her swift brakes!

The ruthless claws of covid

The invisible enemy that flutters airborne targeting its next carrier,
As the population enters hibernation in their homes with face masks as a barrier.
Originating from a bat its mutations are rapid attacking humans at incredible speed,
As we succumb to coughing, loss of taste and burning temperatures the virus succeeds.
For every surface and item is sanitised as a precaution limiting further transmission,
Even post and food isn't immune from its merciless progression.
For new restrictions were imposed to limit spread announcing a curfew by ten,
The mantra 'stay at home' was reiterated joining in solitude the silence of Big Ben.
Next came household bubbles allowing pairing for some social support to be provided,
Followed by social distancing of two metres to keep the silent carriers divided.
Daily exercise was permitted to stretch the legs and preserve mental sanity,
However homeschooling did bring some to the brink of insanity.
Social events dwindled from calendars with weddings

becoming small affairs,
With hospital workers permitted parking on site waiving the parking fares.
Supermarkets were stripped bare as staple foods were stashed and toilet rolls hoarded,
Exposing mankind to prioritise self-preservation as selfless NHS workers were applauded.
Every day the death toll incrementally increased as hundreds fell victim to the virus's brutality,
With national lockdowns curbing the spread to condense it to certain localities.
For travel was restricted and the seeds of new career pathways were planted,
For covid was a humbling experience reminding us that health was not to be taken for granted.

The gilded cage of a doctor

Exhausted, hungry and emotionally depleted is the least of my concerns,
As we wheel the next patient to emergency theatre with staff scuttling back in return.
Brief introductions are exchanged as gowns and gloves are donned,
With that we begin to toil away working above and beyond.
With that the final count confirms all is accounted for as gloves are removed,
ward staff are instructed on the new admission and the handover is approved.

A+E referrals build up as new emergencies await attention,
Each with an ailment or gaping wound stacked with gauze for blood retention.
With that I begin suturing, knitting flesh back together in a methodical fashion,
Like a rag doll I bring the edges back together diminishing the last of my compassion.
Finishing up I return to the ward where patients are fast asleep,
Whereas I stand like a lifeless zombie at the mercy of my loathsome bleep.
Brief greetings are exchanged as nurses request prescriptions to be activated and fluid charts to be completed,

as with each passing hour saline bags are progressively depleted.

With that I welcome a three a.m. lunch break with a much needed caffeine drink,
As I spear through cold chicken pasta and shovel it in big mouthfuls in a blink.
The steaming coffee quenches my parched throat as I soak in the short-lived silence.
As in those few moments I seek refuge from the chaos of overwhelming medical science.

For as a doctor one becomes a selfless creature awaiting to service those in need,
All the while burdening their wings with everyone's pressing plead.
For once the shift comes to an end the cavalry arrives with replenishing reserves,
As a pecking order is established and the baton passed on to the next awaiting to serve.

The celebrity imposter

Fashion before comfort they say as I squeeze myself into a tight dress,
Little does anyone know that just moments before I was vomiting up my Eton mess.
For a thin waist is desired to showcase my petite hourglass figure,
Who cares if the shadow of girl beneath is mentally disfigured.

With that my designer begins her task of sewing me into the gown,
As I pick at the beadwork around my bosom with a frown.
"Done" she announces as I subconsciously look at my flesh exposed,
For surely on a winter's night a full-length gown would be better imposed.

With that, high heels and matching jewellery is adorned,
For I gather my belongings as my compressed toes moaned.
At that the limousine arrives as my PA blithers away the event's itinerary.
Arriving I adjust my seating for a smooth emergence as I hear my introduction in the commentary.
At that the door opens and I gracefully come forth to be bathed in glittering lights,

As privacy fades and judgements are passed it exposes a hidden fight.
I meander through the paparazzi as the crowd's criticism drowns out the dwindling applause,
for any compliments falls on deaf ears as media await for any mishaps to bring everything to a deafening pause.
For creating a spectacle of oneself is the nightmare we all envisage,
Where one prays the media preserves one's dignity whilst they capture their controversial image.
In that moment in the multitude of flashes and sea of voices one feels so isolated,
As one is surrounded by acquaintances on the red carpet with crazed admirers behind stands so clearly segregated.
So for those that crave the limelight, remember that the more your climb up the wall of fame,
The more detached you become from your loved ones becoming a lifeless doll standing in a golden frame.

Autumn

Autumn, the season of hot drinks, knitted mittens and pumpkin pies.
As summer holidays near a close, and alarm clocks are despised.

The rustle of forsaken leaves held hostage to the whistling winds and bellowing breeze,
the crystal blue skies shrouded by casting clouds that give the sun a tight squeeze.
The flowers once in full bloom competing with its peers, now breathing its last breath,
for accepting its lingering lifespan it welcomes its upcoming beaconing death.

The excitement of children brandishing their new uniforms, climbing the academic ladder,
as nursery teachers pray that parents parted wisdom on how to control their persistent bladders.
The chime of the school bell dictates the closing of creaking school gates,
as welcoming teachers usher students into queues to register the new intakes.

Carved pumpkins each a witness to the skill of its artist's spear,

hollowed out to its mere skeleton emanating a sense of foreboding fear.
The chatter of children dressed in their ghoulish attire impressing its streets inhabitants,
amassing scrumplish sweets for their finagling ways proving Halloween to be extravagant!

The illuminating bangs of fireworks each casting its silhouettes on its enchanted audience.
Even Guy Fawkes would be impressed at his legacy's rippling effect and snigger at his experience.
The misting of windscreens and crunching of grass as Jack Frost will soon rear his impish head,
for his mischievous magic and innate talents are there to flamboyantly spread.

A season of change that relinquishes the warmth of summer bliss,
 to wither away and depart winter's bitter cold kiss!

The skeletons of Halloween

A night of macabre and a celebration of terror as youngsters showcase their ghoulish attire,
Knocking door to door gathering treats to gobble singing "trick or treat" as they acquire.
Carving pumpkins to a mere shell creating jack-o-lanterns to ward spirits away.
For Halloween was the day when the barrier between the physical world and the spirit world went astray.
The origin of Halloween can be chased back to ancient Celtic culture,
Where the pagan celebration of Samhain marking the end of harvest season had bonfires rupture.
For they resorted to disguises with masks hoping to frighten the evil spirits floating,
Enticing them with food left on the doorstep they left gloating.

For even witches were feared by many depicted with pointed noses and flying brooms,
With warts and cackling laughter they glide in their draping robes distilling gloom.
For the original pioneering witches were widows, spinsters and natural healers.
Tortured to confess to their wickedness's for being the devil's dealers,

executed mercilessly by hanging or burning to the stake,
The numbers decreased as fewer cauldrons brewed mandrakes!
The Salem witch trails allowed the accused to voice their innocence,
But with tension high and smallpox rife the jury were not pawns of beneficence.
For in the modern day we lavish in apple bobbing, playing pranks and visiting spooky destinations,
All the while our soul sisters lament over their mockery, falling victim to an ancient brutal annihilation.

The old sparks of Bonfire Night

The squeals and bangs illuminated the sky as each firework painted the heavens in its own style,
But for some sparklers are magic wands held outright as they mutter spells of glory and vile.
For Bonfire Night is the awaited night where numerous fireworks are stockpiled,
First we have the rockets that can shoot up high with speed for miles.
Next we have the crackling Roman Candle that bursts into a shower of shining stars,
Followed by the Fountain that explodes magnificently without the audible scars.
The Mine is the mightiest with the loudest bangs it penetrates the darkness with its flooding flashes,
Only for the cake to work in unison with its peers to ignite a sequence of soaring splashes.
But my favourite is the Catherine Wheel that sparks in a pinwheel fashion chasing its tail,
It crackles in sorrow in memory of Saint Catherine mocking Emperor Maxentius's fail.
For the strength of her unfaltering Christian faith lead to her brutal decapitation,
For torturing on the wheel proved to be a disappointment to its unrivalled reputation.
The spark of Bonfire Night can be traced back to the failed

Gunpowder plot,
Led by a devout Catholic Robert Catesby wishing to overthrow the protestant squat,
It targeted King James the first who supported the religious persecution.
Choosing a cellar situated beneath the House of Lords was perfect for the conspiracy execution.
However an anonymous letter leaked to the King's chief minister arouse suspicion,
As vaults were searched revealing thirty-six barrels of gunpowder awaiting ignition.
With Guy Fawkes the known explosive expert onsite beholding fuses and matches,
Leading to his inhumane arrest as conspirators names were confessed in batches.
For they were sentenced to hanging followed by dismemberment of their bodies in splatters,
For plotting against the powerful King was no laughing matter.
So the next time you admire a fireworks vibrance and breath in the exuberance,
Spare a thought to those found guilty of treason for attempting to overthrow tyrannical rule with illuminance.

Winter

Winter, the season of Christmas festivities, snow blizzards and hibernation.
For coughs and colds linger as the flu virus flaunts its crafty mutations.

The muffled crunch of snow as fresh shoe prints tarnish its unflawed beauty.
Its feathery dusting glazing the bare tree limbs that once provided shelter as its humane duty.
Trees now merely reduced to carcasses unable to sustain themselves.
They glance to their fellow comrades while the last leaves shudder from their shelves.

The withered vines of plants wince under winter's wrath, shivering to their bare bones,
 whilst squirrels scurry purposely gathering acorns entombed beneath the stones.
Hedgehogs curl into the foetal position parading its prickly exterior to predators,
hoping to survive this treacherous season to outsmart its fellow competitors.

Amongst this obliterating darkness, the faint glimmer of Christmas lights glow,

reminding those around us that the festive season is due to bestow.
The reenactment of nativity plays, allows those to rejoice in their unfaltering faith.
As fireplaces awakened, with dancing flames sending up their smoky wraith.

Decorative trees line the streets as choir groups unanimously recite classical songs.
Televisions regurgitate Christmas movies each keeping the merry spirit strong.
With the promise that on leaving a carrot, mince pie and an alcoholic beverage,
one might be dealt a better hand in gifts this year as leverage.

The frantic unwrapping of presents as the receiver reveals the hidden treasure,
while the sender watches in anticipation to decipher if it's true to its measure.
The aroma of a freshly cooked turkey dinner brings all to the overflowing dinner table,
as the dreaded sprouts are handed around like a Russian roulette, they begin a Christmas fable.

Once the indulgence and exuberance of the meal is devoured,
a reassuring bliss settles as the last of the pots and pans are scoured.
They look around to appreciate the reuniting of ageing generations,
as in that moment with their belly full and family near it dawns there could be no better location.

Christmas Eve in the North Pole

It was the final month of the year and the North Pole was never more animated,
For it was the Christmas month where every pillar and post was decorated.
With snowflakes cascading in a flurry, each layer encircling the last like a blindfold.
But one house in particular emitted a warm glow with mistletoe wreathed around the threshold.
For this was the residence of Santa Claus that stood proud and tall,
With dawn approaching the alarm sounds awaking Santa from his slumber with a jingle bell call.

Fumbling up he assesses his surroundings as his head elf appears from thin air,
"Morning, Santa, the final Nice list is ready," skimming the scroll he tames his rugged hair.
"Yes correct but George Smith better be nice to his sister next year," he nods.
With that the elf returns to the workshop to work diligently with his squad.

As toys are polished and wrapped away each is christened with its unique name.
For each gift is fitting for its child spanning from princess

dolls to video games.
The elves dutifully toil away with their ears standing proud from their hats,
As they serve in servitude to Santa grateful for the warm clothes that are better than tats!
For they did occasionally pull the odd prank on the reindeers when Santa's back was turned,
But Mrs Claus was not to be fooled, quick to pinch ears for those parties concerned.

Santa in the meantime brushed his teeth as his dentist was forever noticing new cavities,
For all those mince pies and sugar canes were scoffed in abundance without concern for any formalities.
With his dressing gown wrapped tight his nose sniffs some freshly made oatmeal,
However to his dismay his breakfast was a yellow grapefruit freshly peeled.
"Now don't give me that look, Santa, you heard what the doctor said fruit is good for you," Mrs Claus rebuked.
He reluctantly ate his breakfast swallowing mouthfuls holding back feigned puke.
"Now Santa, your suit is washed and ironed, try and go easy on the whiskey this time as it clings on your suit like poignant perfume,
Also remember to take your muddy boots off in the hallway otherwise I'll be chasing you with the broom,"
Santa chuckled as he remembered his generous drinks last year was nothing short of a pub crawl,
He was quite impartial to the odd glass of sherry but somehow always ended up in a merry sprawl.

With that Mrs Claus went to the stables to feed the reindeers,
Who always had a hearty appetite as Santa's loyal musketeers.
Dancer and Prancer were always first to jump up in their elegance,
Followed by Comet jumping up like a lightning bolt in confidence.
Whilst Dasher ploughed through next showering his comrades in snow,
Vixen shaking his head in annoyance devoured her oatmeal in one go!
Blitzen however was first to finish licking his bowl clean,
Followed by Donner whose thunderous gallop made the surroundings a trampoline.
Cupid however savoured her meal blinking through her long lashes she nuzzled Mrs Claus's hand,
Then was Rudolph who was Mrs Claus's favourite,
sprinkling extra cinnamon to make sure his was far from bland.

Santa in the meantime oiled the wheels of his sleigh and gave the woodwork a good polish,
For every year his sleigh and flying reindeers was a sight to astonish.
On entering the workshop the elves were working full throttle with sacks piled high,
"Santa the sacks are ready, labelled with street names and numbers, ready to fly,"
With that Santa hoisted each up and loaded his sledge ready

to deliver.
With the reindeers approaching he assigned the order, with Rudolph last to arrive in a quiver.
"It's okay, Rudolph, I believe you will lead us safely tonight,
For the wind and snow is a little murky,
But don't worry a belly full of carrots, mince pies and milk will soon get you perky!"
With a hearty laugh Santa amounted his sleigh, brushing a quick kiss on Mrs Claus's cheek,
As after all her turkey dinners and scrumptious puddings were responsible for his rounded physique!

The uninvited Icy guest

A blizzard of snow was predicted as a white blanket shrouds the town,
Each fleck of snow glides down on the rooftops gifting each its own icy crown.
Cloaking the greenery it engulfs anything it befalls,
For snow is the awaited guest at every winter fall.

Commuters look on as train lines are cancelled with electrical faults reported.
The buses delayed as their tyres squelch through the icy roads with their progress thwarted.
Workers scrap tirelessly the glazed frost on their windscreens hoping to make up for lost time,
As traffic builds up with each vehicle churning up the grit into a sluggish grime.

However all was not doom and gloom as little children open their curtains and rejoice,
For they rub their hands in glee as they clamber down the stairs with excitement laced in their voice.
For snowmen, snow angels and snowball fights are to be anticipated,
As after all snow is no less than a novelty for those infatuated.

Parents listen with eager ears for possible school closures as radios mutter,
For making a futile quest to school will make anyone no less than a nutter!
Children stand in limbo silently praying for a school snow day to prevail,
As their parents swipe endlessly hoping for an update via email.

At thus phones chimes announcing that school closures are inevitable,
Leading children to scramble into their snow boots to contest whose snow art skill is incredible.
Parents look on as last minute childcare arrangements are compiled,
As children dash out leaving muddy footprints as the crisp soft snow is defiled.

Children run in circles as their breath creates mists of clouds in their wake,
As tired residents navigate their concealed driveways with a rake.
But amongst these is the elderly that hug their clothes tight around their chest,
For their shopping errands will have to wait as they fall victim to a house arrest!
Instead they seek solace drinking hot tea near their fireplace,
As their joints ache and teeth chatter at a quivering pace.

For snow although a short-lived visitor that has a selfless character,

its innocent complexion and icy persona is enough to test any barrister!
But as the day continues the sun beams down shrivelling it to its bare bones,
No less than a distant memory as snowmen are reduced to a pile of stones!

Postpartum mum

Mirror mirror on the wall,
who is this lifeless zombie that once stood tall?

Her hair ragged like Medusa's mane,
her mind burdened in emotional pain.
Battling fear, anger and disbelief,
her weary eyes fatigued in relief.
Searching for familiarity in the woman standing before thee.
Surely this neglected stranger is not me?

Her hands graze the stretch marks that mar her abdomen,
 a testament to the human it housed there for nine months.
Amen!
With each kick and heartbeat signifying the birth of a new life.
Her fingers caress her bandage as she reminisces over the surgical knife.

She feels the fullness in her breasts, a primitive means of nourishment to her child,
but yet this concept was foreign to her… Surely my maiden bosoms couldn't be so wild?
When did her body transition to service a little being was bewildering,
yet she has felt this innate strength within her simmering.

She feels a wetness in-between her thighs,
 as her drenched towels soak up their awaited prize.
Trickling blood that once nestled her newborn, now made redundant and flowing in despair.
She wonders to herself when will she feel her habitual self, as surely motherhood isn't this unfair?

She hears a cry not so far belonging to the newest guest, instinctively her body responds, as she nurtures her to her chest.
In that moment, a reluctant acceptance dawned where Demeter lamented over Persephone's loss,
she too had awakened the potent maternal goddess within that would become the Boss!

First day back

Nappies, change of clothes and breastmilk pouches all stocked in her rucksack,
for today was her child's nursery day and her first day back in her hatchback.
She wrestles the baby into the car seat and lets out an exasperated sigh,
thinking how much has changed since her last work goodbye.

On arrival at the nursery, the staff welcome its newest addition,
as she hands over her child in immaculate condition.
As she leaves she feels her heart lurch as her eyes well,
ridden with guilt and sorrow her mind dwells.

She parks up at work and changes into her scrubs,
hoping her little one will settle well into the evening clubs.
She musters up her courage as a competent clinician she must be,
whilst scanning clinical notes she remembers she forgot to pee.

As the morning pervades, she half-heartedly greets her fellow workers,
as the patient queues dwindle down to the last few lurkers.

She opens her bag in search for her pre-made lunch,
only to realise she left it at home during her morning hasty brunch.

Coffee and a chocolate biscuit will have to suffice,
for she needs to pump her breasts as a lunchtime sacrifice.
As the clinic continues, she glances at her phone for any messages,
relieved as "no messages" beams, she finishes the last of her beverages.

Hurriedly she packs up her belongings, as the day comes to an end,
the night setting in as she drives back before the darkness descends.
She rushes to the nursery to find her baby swatting imaginary flies,
as her baby jumps and yelps in excited surprise.

Oblivious to the spectators she embraces her to her chest,
for that warmth and innocent being knows no better nest.
She leaves to go home looking half a sight,
as now she beholds what truly will keep her up all night!

The birth of a little boss

So it began with a little angel swaddled in blankets with pink balloons marking her arrival,
As everyone baths her in love and admiration, the mother has the task of ensuring her survival.
So she begins sanitising clothes, bottles and bedding for her little cherub,
For she works on every worktop and surface ensuring all fall victim to a good scrub.

However as time passes her little baby lavishes the unconditional attention,
Her regular diaper servicing and untimely demands were always a source of apprehension.
For babies are poor communicators and impatient beings with specific needs,
where one can only stipulate whether it is time for their next feed.

If that doesn't succeed we go back through the process of elimination,
Wet diaper? too hot? too cold? trapped wind? would be the next consideration.
For if all else fails a little snuggle and warmth becomes the default to achieving liberation.
For what one does to soothe an irrational being has no limits

from driving aimlessly to rocking for an endless duration.
Then comes the fragmented sleep where the baby ensures its presence is audible to all in a five mile radius,
For the wailing cries and thrusting legs is nothing short of the work of a genius.
For children are secret masterminds dancing us to their whims,
For they know which strings to pull to having us playing horses on all four limbs!

So parents we are merely puppets at the mercy of our little masters,
For a puckered face has us on our knees and emptying wallets no faster.
To serve these beings becomes a lifelong project as they carve a place in our hearts,
From terrorising our beds, making us cook to their tastes and participating in their fancy arts.
For in the early hours of the morning I pace the halls hostage to my child's cries,
I do wonder if I have become victim to Stockholm syndrome as truly that would be of no surprise!

The musings of a dad

My senses awakened with every gulp, as the caffeine chases away the fringes of my sleep,
For as a parent lie ins are a forbidden luxury as my daughter belts baa baa black sheep.
I hastily sit eating the leftover crusts of my daughter's toast reminiscing over my past,
Regretting the fact that I didn't cherish those carefree days as good things never last.
From arm wrestles, stag dos, frontside seating at football matches to inebriated nights out,
To building enchanted fortresses and playing tea parties pouring tea from a magical spout!

Surely the joyful adventures of parenthood is a myth each generation tells the next to secure future offspring,
As the fear of not having a legacy to leave behind has us all pushing playground swings.
But all is not lost as tomorrow we will he attending the circus with lots of juggling clowns,
Surely that will provide some moments of salvation as I let my children run rampage in town.
For candyfloss and toffee popcorn is the perfect snack to offer enthralled kids,
That will no doubt have them dancing with imaginary monkeys until sleep closes their eyelids.

The loss of a little friend

A blood curdling scream has me paralysed on the spot as my daughter sobs,
For surely not another visit to A+E for an injury that will have me childproofing doorknobs!
Any more casualties will have social services giving us a knock.
"Daddy Freddie isn't swimming," she blubbers in shock.
For what does one expect from a fish that was a free prize at the funfair,
Its demise was always one to be awaited for likely before I sprouted another grey hair.
"There there, Hun, I'm sure Freddie is just sleeping," I improvise on the spot.
"No, Daddy, he's not breathing bubbles," she wails crawling into her cot.
With that I struggle to fathom how to describe death to an innocent child,
For how to comprehend that something she values has departed before its time is wild.
"Daddy, he's gone, he was my secret keeper and friend and now he's passed on."
I rub her back gently cursing myself for not changing the water before he was gone.
"It's OK, Hun, Freddie is in a better place now with his family and friends," I splutter,

"Daddy, you don't know that! What if they don't play nice with him," she stutters.
She continues to bellow in agony pulling at my heartstrings for only if I could reverse back time.
For giving short-lived delicate fish to children should be a punishable crime.

"There there, Hun, we will forever have a place for Freddie in our hearts,
But for now we must let him move on to his next home up in the sky he departs,"
To my amazement my daughter empties her personally decorated jewellery box,
"This, Daddy, should be big enough for his burial so he can rest in peace safe from the wandering fox."

For once I am thrown back as I struggle to fathom my daughter's words,
When did funerals and burials become a necessity for little fish was unheard.
So we begin digging a grave next to the flowerbed with perfect view of the sky,
So little Freddie may have an ample view of the sun whilst admiring the pretty flowers growing high.
"Bye, Freddie, I will always remember you, you will live forever in my heart," she whispers in a murmur,
Tossing a handful of soil she cowers away holding onto her mum a little firmer.
As a father your role is to protect from all harm, but how can we shelter our brood from life's truths?
As I stand totally helpless in that moment I can't help but

ponder how to console a pining youth.

"OK, Hun, how about some ice cream? What will help you feel better?" I quiz.

"A new pet rabbit called fluffy with brown patches would be nice," she spurts in a whiz.

"Done, Hun, we will drive to the pet store after lunch," I grin giving due penance to the deceased.

Only for my wife to roll her eyes "Better dig another grave in preparation as the stray fox will enjoy his next feast!"

Rules

"Catch catch, Mummy," she shrieks, as the ball glides
through the air in the diner.
I catch it abruptly thinking when did I start taking
instructions from a minor.
"No throwing indoors," I reprimand, as she puckers her lip
in irritation.
"Silly rules," she mutters under her breath as I grind my
teeth in frustration.

"Mummy, who makes rules?" she inquires without
hesitation,
gathering my thoughts I contemplate a plausible explanation.
My mind whizzes with thoughts originating back to the ten
commandments,
Blasphemy, infidelity, morality, theft were Moses sacred
enchantments.
But these concepts seemed too complicated and mature,
for a child that still needs her fluffy teddy bear to feel secure.

I smile sheepishly as I cast my mind back to my
anthropology class,
my mind recalls the Magna Carta compiled to protect the
mass.
Restricting the King from exploiting his power by
constructing the law,

but to describe this script to a child seemed archaic as she slurps through her straw.

I take a bite of my burger hastily as a police officer walks along,
That's it! "The police. They punish those that do wrong."
"No, Mummy. They don't make the rules they reinforce them," she gives me a troll stare,
I raise my eyebrows thinking when did my daughter become so aware.

Again my mind goes back to the drawing board, I reminiscence over my past transgressions,
my mantra 'rules are meant to be broken' was my favourite childhood confession.
That's it! 'School and educational establishments make the rules!
Teachers educate and deter us, to stop us all becoming a bunch of misbehaving mules'.

She nods deep in thought and with a pensive expression,
She takes several bites of her chicken nuggets in quick succession.
"But, Mummy, why is it you tell me not to talk with my mouth full,
And not to put my elbows on the table," she muffles with cheeks taut like a bull.

I roll my eyes thinking how to explain social etiquette to my brood,
For not following social norms and good manners would be

rude.

"Well, honey, that's just called being polite and showing courtesy to your host."

I finish my burger and wipe my hands, as she munches the last of her toast.

For that was a deep conversation to shoulder whilst drinking only a diet coke,
Thankful that she was content with my answers as that was the last she spoke.
Explaining parliament, legal jurisdiction and social norms would have been hard,
For somethings are best to humour for now so they enjoy the childhood they are so quick to discard.

On our return she glimpses her father tapping away on his iPad immersed in work.
Excitedly he jumps up, catching his elbow he pulls away with a jerk,
"Ouch! Oh Lord," he curses profanity under his breath massaging the area with a sigh.
"No, Daddy, thou mustn't use Gods name in vain," she chastised with her finger held high.

He looks in my direction in amazement with confusion painted on his face,
"We were discussing rules earlier on today," I reply with a quick embrace.
"Oh I'm sure Mummy told you about the seven deadly sins," he says at a pace,
immediately my child's interests piques as she jumps into his

lap with grace.

So, he begins "Pride, greed, wrath, envy, sloth, gluttony and lust are the seven sins."
Swiftly I take this opportunity to brew a cuppa and open a box of chocolate thins.
As with Christmas upon us, we all know that gluttony is inevitable,
but alas let thou without sin cast the first stone, for a little transient sin is negligible.

The fable of inferno

"Daddy, why is it you tell me to be a good girl and not to hurt others?" she inquires with childlike innocence.
I reply, "For have you not heard that those who do bad will go to hell if they stray the path of maleficence."
She looks at me quizzingly, her eyes beseeching me to divulge more,
For at this age their brains are sponges awaiting to store.

So I begin, trickling my knowledge into my child so she too can thrive,
"Once a upon a time, my friend Dante found himself lost in the woods, searching for a path to survive,
On embarking on a mountain he finds his path obstructed by three beasts,
Pushing him back into the sinister darkness they lick their lips for their next feast.
Luckily to his aid comes a comrade called Virgil sent by good spirits to accompany his passage,
So they make their way to the gates of hell passing indecisive people seeking salvage.
For hell has nine circles each ascending to different levels of wickedness,
So that the punishment is just for the crime it preys on their weaknesses."

My child looks at me in terror with fear distilled within her eyes,
She whispers, "Daddy but isn't hell Satan's home, the devil we all despise?"
"Yes indeed, he is at its centre, but first we come across those in limbo who failed to be baptised,
Then those who succumbed to lust swaying in the bellowing winds forever being chastised.
Next we come across overindulgent folk that didn't know how to curb their appetites grovelling in mud,
For that leads us to the greedy fellows who hoarded possessions, forever clattering weights to one another with a thud.
Next the fifth circle we come across the wrathful brawling in the swampy waters, snarling and gurgling subpar,
With that they travel by boat to descend lower as the next circles are far."

"Blessed by an angel they are permitted entry to the deeper circles into the city of Dis,
Next they see those that denied faith's teachings imprisoned in burning tombs in dark abyss.
Next they climb down the fallen rocks to the seventh circle which houses the half-bull half-man Minotaur,
With gentle persuasion and a price they are permitted entrance with candour.
Here they see those that committed murder boiling in a river of crimson blood flowing,
Not far is a forest of gnarled trees embodying those who departed on their own terms mauled by birds clawing.
And next to this is the scorching desert with searing rain

falling on the burning sand,
Scalding those that utter the God's name in vain and those that take advantage of the weak to gain the upper hand."

"So that's why Mummy has the penny swear jar at home, she intends to bribe Satan?" she inquires,
"Maybe," I smirk thinking a handful of pennies will hardly attract a single buyer.
"Then they take flight on the back of a winged creature to the eighth circle funnelling into a series of ten ditches,
In this circle those that commit fraud are whipped by demons for seducing or exploiting others to gain riches."
At this my daughter yawns. "Daddy this story is a little long," she says as her eyebrows furrow.
At this I take the hint as maybe going through all ten ditches maybe a little too thorough.

"So they pass those that told false flatteries to others, barking away in human dung."
With this my daughter cracks a laugh, "Better tell Mummy her lemon chicken isn't so delicious Daddy," she bites her tongue.
Rolling my eyes, "So the rest of the circle has several layers, but to name a few,
The fortune tellers walk backwards in line with their heads twisted as punishment for their prophesying views.
The corrupt politicians rest in a lake of bubbling tar attacked by demons silencing their plight.
Thieves reside not so far, bitten by snakes and reptiles they cower away in fright.
Finally we come to the ninth circle, where those that commit

treachery lie beneath the frozen ice of the lake,
Each at differing levels reflecting the extent of their mistakes.
And there at the centre lies Satan with his three heads, munching on the bones of sinners,
 as imprisoned in the frozen lake he must remain cursed to his distasteful dinners."

With that my daughter scrunches up her nose as cannibalism isn't everyone's cup of tea.
"Daddy, did your friend get out alive? How did he flee?"
"With that my friend Dante in a panic rushes to leave, escaping via Satan's crotch they scramble out at speed, climbing up the rocks to ascend back to humanity they are relieved to be free before Satan's next feed!"

I look down to see my daughter's confusion, deep in thought she mutters,
"Daddy, I have a confession to make, I don't like your macaroni and cheese," she stutters.
"That's okay, honey, thank you for your honesty," I smile wondering if cooking was ever my forte,
"Now next to tell Mummy her singing is atrocious, and she definitely is not the next Beyoncé."
I smile to myself thinking how Dante's work has many multifaceted interpretations,
But to the simplest of minds it's more than sufficient to fill them with trepidation.

My clever brother Tom

My clever brother Tom, is my idol and fountain of knowledge and wisdom,
For he is nothing short of a human encyclopaedia always quick to treat any symptom.
He's my protector and strength always happy to take the fall should Mum get cross,
But nonetheless he's always let me win arm wrestles so I'm never at a loss.

"Tom, what's a newsagents?" I ask as we walked past an illuminated store,
"Oh that, Jake, is the headquarters for undercover spy agents from war,
where they exchange secrets of victories and grizzly galore."
With that I always saluted fervently the spies exiting every day from the door.

"Tom where did I come from?" I quiz as his mum turned bright red in the sunlight,
"Oh, Jake, we plucked you up from the garden, you didn't half give us a fright!
But because you were cute we thought we might as well keep you for now."
That made sense I nod as Dad was always digging in the garden with his plough.

"Tom, what's a lollipop lady?" I ask as the traffic comes to a standstill,
"Oh, Jake, she gives lollipops to those that are good at skipping across for their great skill."
So from that day on I always did an animated skip leaping extra high to the sky,
That always succeeded to make her smile but in terms of a lollipop that she is yet to supply.

"Tom, what does that 'To let' sign mean?" I ask as we pass the bus stop,
"Oh, Jake, that's to say someone stole their toilet last night in that shop,
so should anyone come across an abandoned toilet to contact that number."
"OK, Tom, I'll keep my eyes peeled," so I did keeping an eye open even in my deepest slumber.

"Tom, what is a car boot sale?" I ask as we pass a road sign on route to buying tootsie fruits.
"Oh, Jake, it's an adult version of real car dodgems, where if you lose they give you the boot."
With that I took a note everyday of all those signs that we passed,
So that when I'm older I'll show them Jake's racing skills are ones to broadcast!

"Tom, why is Mum taking me to get injections?" I splutter
"Oh, Jake, that is how they implant little chips inside us, keeping track of what we mutter."

It's safe to say that the doctor never saw a tantrum of that nature before,
For with the aid of three nurses I was pinned down on all four.

"Tom, why does Daddy say I'm not allowed in the attic?"
"For, Jake, that is where the monsters and ghosts live, forever arguing they are dramatic!"
With that I scuttled into my room far away from the frightful ghouls,
Little did I know that's where Tom stored his prized possessions for why was I so easily fooled.